PRIMARY SOURCES

★★★★★★★★★★★★★★★★★★★ OF ★★★★★★★★★★★★★★★★★★★
IMMIGRATION AND MIGRATION
★ IN AMERICA™ ★

IMMIGRANTS AND
THE WESTWARD EXPANSION

Tracee Sioux

The Rosen Publishing Group's

PRIMARY SOURCE

New York

To my brother, Klint Arley Johnson, a saint

Published in 2004 by The Rosen Publishing Group, Inc.
29 East 21st Street, New York, NY 10010

First Edition

Editor: Rachel O'Connor
Book Design: Emily Muschinske
Layout Design: Mike Donnellan

On the cover: Detail of *Westward the Course of Empire Takes Its Way* (Mural Study, U.S. Capitol) 1861, by Emanuel G. Leutze.

Photo Credits: Cover, p. 11 (top) Smithsonian American Art Museum, Washington, DC/Art Resource, NY; p. 4 Library of Congress Geography and Map Division; p. 7 (top) © Corbis; pp. 7 (bottom), 8 (right and bottom) Independence National Historical Park; p. 7 (right) Réunion des Musées Nationaux/Art Resource, NY; p. 8 (top) Yale Collection of Western Americana, Beinecke Rare Book and Manuscript Library; pp. 11 (bottom), 12 (bottom), 15 (bottom), 19(top) © Hulton/Archive/Getty Images; pp. 12 (top), 15 (right), 16, 20 © Bettmann/Corbis; p. 15 (top) Lowell Georgia/Corbis; p. 19 (bottom) © Dale C. Spartas/Corbis.

Sioux, Tracee.
Immigrants and the westward expansion / Tracee Sioux.
    p. cm. — (Primary sources of immigration and migration in America)
Summary: Describes the discovery and settlement of the Western United States by diverse ethnic and religious groups, who came and stayed for widely differing reasons.
Includes bibliographical references and index.
ISBN 0-8239-6824-3 (lib. bdg.) — ISBN 0-8239-8950-X (pbk.)
1. Frontier and pioneer life—West (U.S.)—Juvenile literature. 2. Pioneers—West (U.S.)—History—Juvenile literature. 3. Immigrants—West (U.S.)—History—Juvenile literature. 4. West (U.S.)—History—To 1848—Juvenile literature. 5. West (U.S.)—History—1848–1860—Juvenile literature. 6. West (U.S.)—History—1860–1890—Juvenile literature. 7. United States—Emigration and immigration—History—Juvenile literature. 8. United States—Territorial expansion—Juvenile literature. [1. Frontier and pioneer life. 2. Immigrants—West (U.S.) 3. Pioneers—West (U.S.) 4. West (U.S.)—History—1860–1890.] I. Title. II. Series.
F596 .S53 2004
978'.02'08691—dc21

2002154259

Manufactured in the United States of America

Contents

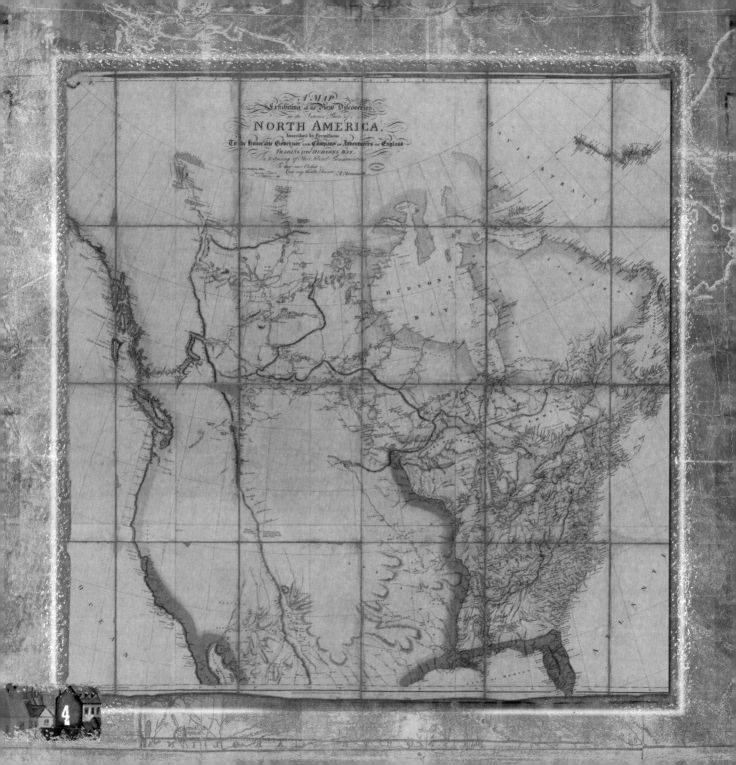

A MAP
Exhibiting all the New Discoveries
in the Interior Parts of
NORTH AMERICA,
Inscribed by Permission
To the Honorable Governor and Company of Adventurers of England
TRADING INTO HUDSONS BAY,
In testimony of their liberal communications

European Immigration

During the 1600s, large numbers of immigrants crossed the Atlantic Ocean to come to America. They came from all over Europe. The Spanish, French, and British were among the first to come.

By the 1800s, the British immigrants had established 13 colonies on the East Coast of America. In 1776, the colonists declared their independence and formed the United States. Later on, the vast land of the West began to interest the immigrants. They were attracted to the West by the opportunities the land and its resources could offer, the possibility of wealth, and a place free from religious persecution.

This 1795 map shows all the new discoveries in North America at the time, including the areas colonized by the British, Spanish, and French. You can see how much of the land in the western parts had yet to be explored.

Obstacles to the West

Americans wanted to claim the West, but first they had to overcome several obstacles. France and Mexico already owned large areas of western territory. In 1803, Jefferson bought the French-owned Louisiana Territory from Napoleon for $15 million, or four cents per 1 acre (0.4 ha). This is known as the Louisiana Purchase. Knowing that the United States owned the land, immigrants felt more secure about moving west.

Mexico owned land west of Louisiana to the Pacific Ocean. After fighting a war with Mexico from 1846 until 1848, the United States gained Texas, California, and New Mexico.

This is a portrait of Thomas Jefferson by Charles Willson Peale. In a speech, Jefferson spoke of America as "a rising nation, spread over a wide and fruitful land, advancing rapidly to destinies beyond the reach of mortal eye."

The Treaty of Guadalupe Hidalgo, signed with Mexico on February 2, 1848, gave the United States the land west of Louisiana.

Above: Napoléon Bonaparte ruled France as first consul and in 1804 became Emperor Napoléon I.

Right: Meriwether Lewis was Thomas Jefferson's first choice to lead the journey to the West. Lewis went on to become governor of the Louisiana Territory in 1808.

Above: William Clark gathered and trained the men for the trip to the West. As well as mapping many of the routes covered on the journey, Clark made sketches of the animal life along the way.

Lewis and Clark

In 1803, U.S. president Thomas Jefferson wanted to find a water route that connected the United States to the Pacific Ocean. His aim was to increase trade in America. Also, he believed that the recently formed United States should stretch from the Atlantic Ocean to the Pacific Ocean. Jefferson sent his secretary Meriwether Lewis to find a northwest passage to the West.

Lewis and William Clark, his co-leader, set off on May 14, 1804, from St. Louis, Missouri. They left with a small group of soldiers known as the Corps of Discovery. It took the group two-and-one-half years to make it to the Pacific and back.

Far Left: *Lewis and Clark recorded maps that showed the progress of their journey. Clark drew this map, which records their route during June 1805.*

Native Americans

To the immigrants who wanted to move and settle throughout the west, the Native American presence on the land was a problem. When the first European immigrants began to colonize the East Coast, there were several million Native Americans in America. Some of the most well-known nations throughout America were the Cherokee, Navajo, Apache, and Sioux. As immigrants began to travel west, they sometimes fought with the Native Americans that they encountered living on the land. Over the years, the fighting resulted in losses to both sides. In the end, however, the immigrants outnumbered the Indians. They forced the Indians off the lands that had been their homes and onto reservations.

Right: *During the 1800s, the Sioux of the North American plains existed by hunting and gathering their food from the land.*

Below: *The Battle of the Little Bighorn in 1876 was one of the greatest losses to the U.S. Army. It was also the last big victory for the Native Americans.*

This photograph from the 1870s is of a Mormon man with his family. They had come to the West to practice their religion in peace.

Below: People migrated to the West in long wagon trains, such as this one showing Mormons near Fort Bridger.

The Mormon Trail

The Mormon Church was founded in 1830 by Joseph Smith in New York State. Many of the first members were English immigrants. One of the most notable waves of migration west was when the Mormons went looking for a home where they could practice their religion without persecution.

A lot of people disagreed with the Mormons' beliefs and persecuted them. After their leader, Joseph Smith, was killed, the Mormons headed west. Led by Brigham Young, they made the hard journey in covered wagons and on foot. Between 1846 and 1869, about 70,000 Mormons moved to the area of Salt Lake City, Utah. Today Utah continues to draw Mormons.

Rushing for Gold

Gold was discovered on the American River near Sacramento, California, in 1848. This began the California gold rush. Word of the discovery spread quickly, and soon the area was flooded with people from every corner of the world. The largest wave of migration during the gold rush hit in 1849. Towns emptied as people headed to California, leaving behind ghost towns. By December 1849, more than 80,000 immigrants had gone west. They had come from the East Coast of America, Mexico, Europe, and China. The population in California nearly tripled because of immigrants seeking their fortunes.

Those who came to California looking for gold set up mining camps along the rivers where gold had been found. Life was usually hard in the camps. The miners lived in leaky tents or log cabins, and food was often scarce.

Right: *This is a modern-day view of the American River, where the first gold pieces were found in 1848.*

AN ACCOUNT OF
CALIFORNIA,
AND THE
WONDERFUL GOLD REGIONS.

A New Arrival at the Gold Diggings.

WITH A DESCRIPTION OF

The Different Routes to California;
Information about the Country, and the Ancient and
Modern Discoveries of Gold;
How to Test Precious Metals; Accounts of Gold Hunters;
TOGETHER WITH MUCH OTHER
Useful Reading for those going to California, or having Friends there.

ILLUSTRATED WITH MAPS AND ENGRAVINGS.

BOSTON:
PUBLISHED BY J. B. HALL, 66 CORNHILL.
For Sale at Skinner's Publication Rooms, 60½ Cornhill.

Above: *A gold-mining manual, published in 1849, promised tips and information about mining gold in California.*

The Homestead Act

Abraham Lincoln was elected president of the United States in 1860. In 1862, Congress passed the Homestead Act, which was meant to encourage migration of U.S. citizens to the West. The government did not want the land it had secured in the West to lay empty. The government feared that if the land was unoccupied, it would be taken by Mexican gangs or by the displaced Native Americans. The Homestead Act allowed citizens to settle on 160 acres (64.8 ha) of unclaimed public land. In return, the settlers would work the land and make improvements. After five years, the settlers would officially own the land.

On May 20, 1862, President Lincoln signed the Homestead Act giving land owned by the government to people for settlement. Families like the one shown here in Custer County, Nebraska, left the East to settle this new land.

Wagon Trains

Traders and explorers who had been to the West returned to their homes full of stories about all the opportunities there. Their tales of the West reached people all over the world. Between 1840 and 1870, more than 300,000 people migrated to the West from the East Coast of America, Europe, China, and Russia.

Early migrating families traveled in covered wagons pulled by oxen or mules. They banded together in wagon trains because they felt safer in groups. One wagon train could consist of anywhere from 30 to 100 wagons. Most trains traveled from 12 to 20 miles (19.3–32.2 km) each day.

To keep safe from wild animals and Indian attacks at night, covered wagons such as these would make a circle and the sleeping migrants would huddle close together.

Most covered wagons had rear wheels with 14 spokes and smaller front wheels with 12 spokes.

The Pacific Railroad

In 1862, Congress passed the first Pacific Railroad Act. Two railroad companies were commissioned to build a railroad that would run from California to Nebraska, meeting somewhere in the middle. The railroad companies found there was a lack of workers. They reluctantly hired some Chinese immigrants who had settled in the West. At first no one believed that these small Chinese men were strong enough for rail work. However, the Chinese skillfully dug tunnels and flattened rock with dynamite. In May 1869, the two railroads met in Utah. A golden spike was hammered into the ground in honor of the achievement.

The Chinese immigrants were paid $1 per day to build the railroad. The white workers were paid $1.50. The Chinese workers were not allowed to be present on the day the golden spike was hammered into the ground.

From Sea to Shining Sea

The expansion of the United States westward is a history marked by bloody wars, big dreams, and fierce determination. John L. O'Sullivan, a political leader, named it Manifest Destiny. The belief was that the United States should expand across North America to the Pacific Ocean. It began in 1804, when Lewis and Clark went on their explorations west. They would tell the Native Americans they encountered that the United States now owned their land. Americans used a variety of methods to take control of the land. They explored it, fought for it, bought it, and settled on it. Under James K. Polk, president from 1845 to 1849, Americans made real the vision that America would stretch "from sea to shining sea."

Glossary

achievement (uh-CHEEV-ment) Something great that is done with hard work.

corps (KOR) A group of soldiers who are trained to perform a special military service.

declared (dih-KLEHRD) Announced officially.

determination (dih-ter-mih-NAY-shun) Being firm in purpose.

dynamite (DY-nuh-myt) A powerful explosive used in blasting rock.

encourage (in-KUR-ij) To give hope, cheer, or certainty.

expansion (ek-SPAN-shun) The widening or opening of an area.

homestead (HOHM-sted) A 160-acre (64.8-ha) piece of public land given by the government to farmers.

immigrants (IH-muh-grints) People who move to a new country from another country.

lured (LOORD) To have drawn with a hint of pleasure or gain.

notable (NOH-tuh-bul) Standing out because of excellence or certain qualities.

obstacles (OB-stih-kulz) Things that are in the way.

persecution (per-sih-KYOO-shun) The act of attacking because of one's race or beliefs.

reluctantly (rih-LUK-tunt-lee) To do something without really wanting to.

reservations (reh-zer-VAY-shuns) Areas of land set aside by the government for Native Americans to live on.

resources (REE-sors-ez) Things that occur in nature and that can be used or sold, such as gold, coal, or wool.

Index

Primary Sources

Cover. *Westward the Course of Empire Takes its Way.* By Emanuel G. Leutze. 1861. Oil on canvas. **Page 4.** A map exhibiting all the new discoveries in the interior parts of North America. Hand-colored map mounted on cloth. Published by A. Arrowsmith. January 1, 1795. **Page 7. Top.** Treaty of Guadalupe Hidalgo. 1848. **Bottom right.** Portrait of Thomas Jefferson. By Charles Willson Peale. 1791. **Right.** Napoléon Bonaparte as King of Italy. By Andrea Appiani (1754–1817). Oil on canvas. **Page 8.** Map # 25. From Clark field maps. 1804–1807. **Page 11.** *The Dog, Chief of the Bad Arrow Points Band, Dakota Sioux.* George Catlin. 1832. Oil on canvas. Smithsonian American Art Museum. Washington, D.C. **Page 12.** Mormon frontier settlement in the Far West. 1870s. **Bottom:** Mormon party near Fort Bridger (circa 1865). William Henry Jackson. Watercolor. 1930s. **Page 15.** Title page from a gold mining manual, *An Account of California and the Wonderful Gold Regions.* 1849. Published by J. B. Hall. **Page 16.** Homestead Act settlers outside their home in Nebraska. Circa 1870–1899. **Page 19.** A wagon train of American homesteaders moves across the open plains. 1885. **Page 20.** Driving the golden spike commemorating the completion of the Union Pacific Railroad at Promontory Summit, Utah. May 10, 1869.

Web Sites

Due to the changing nature of Internet links, PowerKids Press has developed an online list of Web sites related to the subject of this book. This site is updated regularly. Please use this link to access the list: www.powerkidslinks.com/psima/westex/